NOTEWORTHY

Meredith Harrigan

illustrated by Patrick Montanaro

Milne Library Publishing

2025

Published by Milne Library
SUNY Geneseo
1 College Circle
Geneseo, NY 14454

ISBN: 978-1-956862-11-9

Hello Beautiful People!

Thank you for taking the time to read my book. I am excited to share my story with you—it is about my journey to make sense of a challenging experience. My journey isn't over, but I think it's a good time to pause and reflect on how far I've come and what I learned before I move on.

As you'll soon discover, I'm feeling quite inspired these days! I haven't always felt this way. For the last few years, I felt worried, sad, and confused after losing something important to me. How did I get from those feelings to inspired? I got there by taking many little steps and A LOT of notes.

I hope that you find among the pages that follow something informative, inspiring, and, most importantly, **NOTEWORTHY**!

With love,
MERRY

Don't ask the mountain
to move, just take a pebble
each time you visit.
John Paul Lederarch

I had never given my smile much thought until I lost it.

Once it was gone, it was all I could think about.

My smile did so many important things for me. It helped me say hello, make friends, show kindness, and fit in. My smile was big and bright and it shone like gold. It was my favorite personal quality.

I worried that I might never shine again. After losing it, it seemed like everywhere I went, all I could see were people smiling.

I began to feel out of place and I longed to fit in.

I wanted to work through my feelings, so I decided to explore them like a scientist explores the moon.

Before I could start, I needed to find a thinking space that worked for me. I get easily distracted and my house is noisy, especially in the morning, which is when I do my best thinking.

After considering different options, I chose a nearby community park.

Each day I'd wake up early, grab what I needed, tiptoe out of the house, and walk to the park to think.

The first morning at the park was warm and inviting. There were so many places to support my thinking. I chose to start by the park's encouraging sign. I secretly hoped it would make my difficult feelings disappear.

I didn't want to worry, and I wanted to be happy. The sign's message reminded me of a song I knew, so I put on my headphones and started to listen and hum along. When that song was over, the playlist replaced it with another.

Like many people, I was taught that I could do anything, including overcoming struggle so I tried to do just that. I put the song on repeat and started walking. But like the deflated balloon I came across, my spirits couldn't rise, and I wondered why.

Wondering became a new habit for me.

When the silence isn't quiet and it feels like it's getting hard to breathe...

♪

I'll rise up, rise like the day, I'll rise up, rise unafraid...

♫

DON'T WORRY BE HAPPY

All the negative ideas I held about people who don't smile swirled around my thoughts, and I wondered where all those negative ideas came from.

The more I thought, the more I worried and the more deflated I felt.

"What if people think *I'm* grumpy?"

"What if people think *I'm* unfriendly?"

"What if people think *I'm* mean?"

"What if people misunderstand *me*?"

It is loud in my mind today; jumbled up.

Lend me your eyes and I'll change what you see.

I cannot think straight,

no matter how many steps I take,

everything feels so far away.

4

I began to feel overwhelmed by my thoughts and by the longing feeling that made my heart ache.

Trying to push through my feelings seemed to make them stronger, so I tried something different.

I stopped to rest upon a giant rock near the park's entrance. I let a wave of worry wash over me and form tears in my eyes. They dripped slowly down my face, off my chin, onto the rock, and into a crevice where other water had puddled.

I sat and listened and was surprised to hear many of my feelings being sung by others. I felt connected to these singers and began to breathe a bit easier.

When I felt ready, I tried walking again. Listening while wandering became a new habit for me.

♪ When the fire inside that burns so bright begins to grow faded. It can be hard to see the ground on which you stand. Though you may not be afraid of walking in the darkness, you will feel like a stranger in this land. ♪

Wish I could feel amazing, but this is all that I can feel today. ♪

Each morning I awoke eager to connect. I expanded my playlist from singers to scientists, authors, and poets. Each helped me think and feel differently.

One lovely spring morning, when I looked around I saw birds gliding over the willows, almost as if they were dancing to their own music. I stepped off the path and walked toward them. When I arrived, I sat on the grass, watched them dance, lowered my headphones, and listened to them. I began to write down all the things that I was thinking and feeling. This became another important habit for me.

What can you hear?

What can you see?

Who will you be?

Who are you now?

Put down the weight of your aloneness and ease into the conversation

Each day, I continued to explore myself and my surroundings.

One spring morning, when I was walking near the sign. I stepped in a mud puddle. Grumpy about what I had done, I bent down to clean the mud off my shoes. I noticed the whole section of grass in front of the sign was muddy and worn.

I thought back to the day I stood in that spot trying not to worry and I wondered if others had done the same.

It's interestin' that nobody can walk in your shoes but still relate.

When we recognize and accept our difficult feelings and emotions we begin to feel more at peace. When we see that mud is something that can help us grow we become less afraid of it.

DON'T WORR
BE HAPP

With each step I took throughout the park on the gravel terrain, my awareness and curiosity grew, and my loneliness and worry waned.

As spring turned to summer, I continued to listen, wander, note, and wonder.

One early summer morning, picturesque clouds drew my attention to the sky.

I noticed a star shape emerging as the sun peeked from behind them. I had seen many stars before, but this one was different. The bottom points stretched from the sky to the ground like giant spotlights.

Curious what they might illuminate, I began moving toward the light.

The things that change us, if we notice, when we look up sometimes.

9

The spotlights led me to the forest.

I peeked in slowly, one eye at a time and was surprised to see a red rake standing among the trees.

I wondered why someone would want to rake in the forest, especially during the summer when the leaves were still on the trees, or were they using the rake differently?

I started imagining what those other differences might be.

I got a hammer, and a bell, and a song to sing land, its the justice,

I got a I got a all over this hammer of it's a bell of freedom, it's a song about love...

What can you do? What can be done?

The next day I came across the rake again. This time it was lying on the path near a row of interesting trees. Each tree in the row was leaning, almost as if it was reaching for something.

I moved the rake from the path and felt an invitation to use it. Although I liked to do things by myself, I wondered if it could help me navigate the rough terrain.

With the help of the rake, I approached each tree and examined it with curiosity. I noticed that each tree had long roots holding it in place. I wondered what might happen if the roots came undone. Would the tree fall or would it stand tall?

I cleaned the rake and placed it back near the path so it'd be available for the next passerby. I continued walking.

I'm gonna root, I'm gonna rise. I'm gonna dig, I'm gonna reach. Become a higher me

PERFECT IONISM

Help those who cross your pathway, for they are there, and you came this way.

11

As I climbed the park's highest hill, a rabbit crossed the path and hopped into the foliage. I noticed how soft its tail appeared. I peeked in with curiosity hoping to get a better look. I came face to face with tiny flowers. I had never looked at flowers so closely, especially little flowers like these.

The more closely I looked the more vivid their unique details became to me. I began to wonder what I might see if I looked more closely at myself. I also wondered what others might see if they looked closely at me.

What a world it would be if nature compared, if flowers didn't flower, because their neighbours were flowerier.

You belong among the wildflowers ... You belong somewhere you feel free.

Later that summer, as I looked closely at the flowers along the path, I noticed that among them were leaves that resembled hearts. I found this interesting and wondered where else I might see hearts if I expanded my field of vision. I began to see them everywhere.

As summer turned to fall and the leaves began to change, I began to realize that with loss can come gain.

Look for the good

Our job is to love the world

We are billions of beautiful hearts

...may
a flock of colours,
indigo, red, green, and azure
blue come to awaken in you a meadow
of delight.

Each day that fall, I continued to practice my new habits.

I listened, wandered, wondered, and noted. I looked closely at each unique leaf that decorated each tree and how each was changing at its own speed. I'd then climb to the park's peak and admire the landscape's color and beauty.

As the leaves fell from the trees, my attention shifted to the ground. One chilly morning, as I climbed the hill, I noticed that the path had two types of gravel. Under one foot, the gravel was firm, and it was loose under the other. I started to think about all the ways I am like the gravel with different qualities coming together.

Stay gentle, the most powerful thing you can do.

LITTLE SHOE LIBRARY

We're happy, free, confused, and lonely at the same time

Sometimes all that you need is someone who can believe in you more than you do.

...the seed...with the sun's love becomes the rose

One bright and sunny day while searching for hearts along the multifaceted gravel, I noticed my shadow traversing alongside me. I had seen my shadow many times before but I never gave it much thought. Today was different. I saw it everywhere I went. It was on the ground and in the foliage, on the trees and even on the giant rock. I couldn't stop looking at it. I wondered if the extra bright sun made it easier to see.

I felt the sun's warmth on my back, as if it was hugging me. I turned back to look and noticed beams radiating behind me. I thanked the sun for energizing me and providing the light that helped me see myself more clearly.

When you touch a tree or sit at the foot of a tree, you can feel the energy of the tree pervading you. The tree has an energy. It simply stands there, being itself, and that is so refreshing, nourishing, and healing.

One late fall day, as I stood with my shadow stretching tall across the grass, I realized how much more I could see now that the trees had lost their leaves. I looked up, down, and around and found my attention being pulled to the playground. I took off my headphones and heard some of the most beautiful sounds.

Invitations to play, happy humming, kind compliments, and light-hearted laughter warmed the air and my heart like a love song. What people chose not to say also inspired me.

I took an extra deep breath and held it in so the warm air would circulate throughout my body.

to the ones who they can and ride on may they

Here's little think touch the sun the moon to the stars... never put their wings away.

When we see other people who are in good communication

with themselves and others, they inspire us.

19

Sunlight fell and reminded me that life can be so gracious sometimes and I felt like everything around me was connected somehow.

I walked down the hill, rounded the corner, passed the sign, and continued walking the park's circular path.

I began reflecting on the many little moments and interactions that brought me delight and peace during my journey, such as the way the dew-covered gravel shimmers when it connects with the morning sun or the way I felt welcomed by waving willows each day. Or how the tree's extended golden branch looked like a protective wing or how the rain's water droplets on flowers looked like nourishing tears.

And, perhaps most importantly, how a fellow walker's quiet nod to say hello or slight step to the side to make room for me made me feel seen.

We can live in a world
we design

Whoever you are, no matter how lonely, the world offers itself to your imagination.

I couldn't stop thinking about how comfortable I felt when I was in this space walking with my headphones on among my new friends, breathing easily and thinking creatively. I wished I could bring this feeling everywhere and share it with others who are searching for something similar.

I reflected on the songs, poems, and friends' words I had jotted down along the way, and how each was a beautiful pebble in the path I journeyed.

With a new lightness in my heart and pep in my step, I made my way to the pavilion that sits between the willows and playground. Inspired, I placed my notebook on the table and started to dream. I looked around and noticed birds working together to build a nest and children working together to build a castle. I began to wonder what I could build and who would build with me.

I started imagining.

Use your imagination and a tremendous thing will happen.

Then I had an epiphany. Could sharing my experience and the pebbles I collected lessen my weight and bring color to others' paths as they journeyed?

I've been having revelations and I'm gon' let them shine.

"Hey my little evening star, how bright you are."

"The world needs you now. You matter, matter, matter."

With a more open mind, heart, and sensitivity, I made my way to the playground and took a seat on the swing, I leaned forward then sat back, again and again.

With each beat, I breathed in and back out, lifting myself and allowing myself to be lifted.

The higher I flew, the more ready I felt to let myself and others *be*.

People are just as wonderful as sunsets if I can let them be...

from

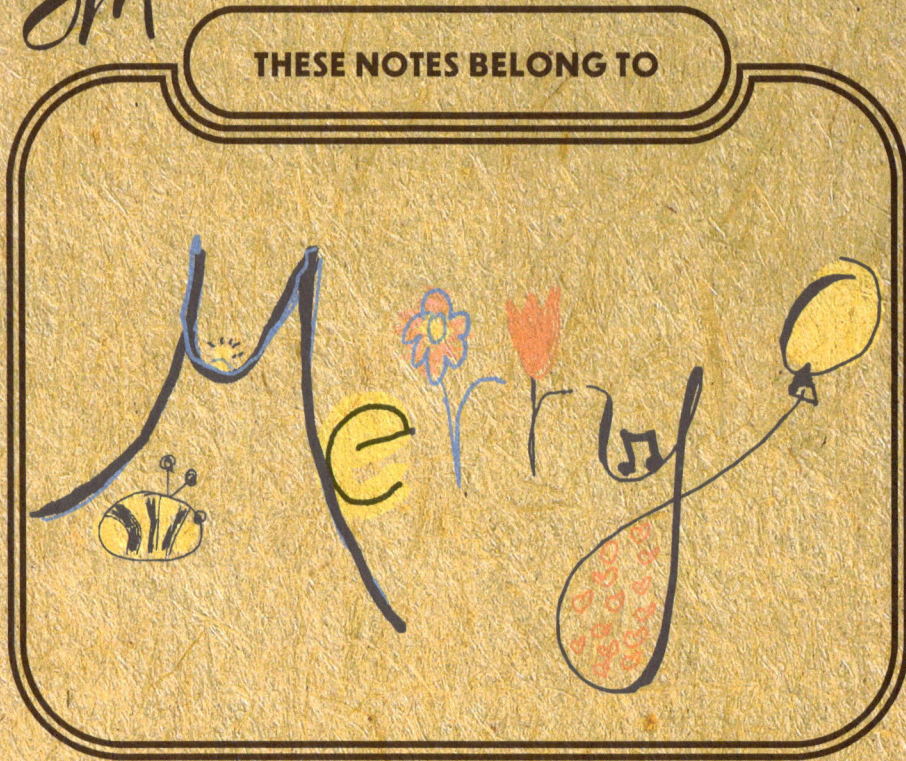

to

you

♥ Today I went to the park again. I spent time sitting on the giant rock near the entrance. I noticed a crevice in the rock was filled with water. I found that interesting.

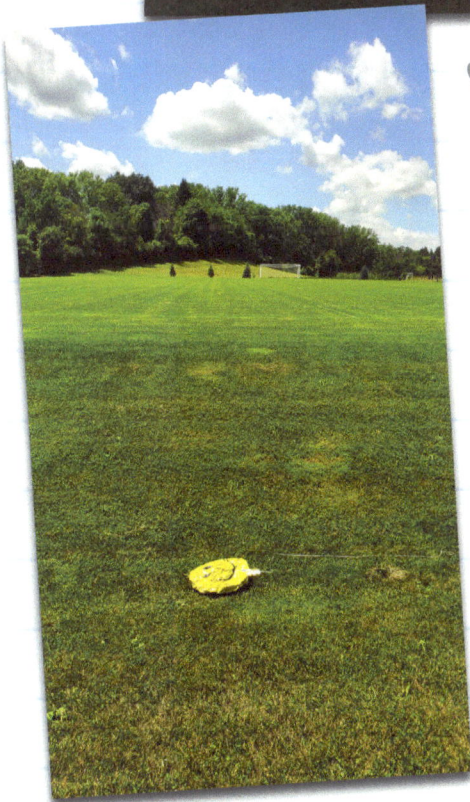

♥ Today I saw a deflated smiley face balloon in the park. It was just lying there in the middle of the grass. I couldn't believe it. Strangely, I felt connected to it.

♥ Today I heard someone ask why I was grumpy. I wasn't. I thought to myself do I have to carry a sign with a happy emoji or one that says "yes, I really am happy!"

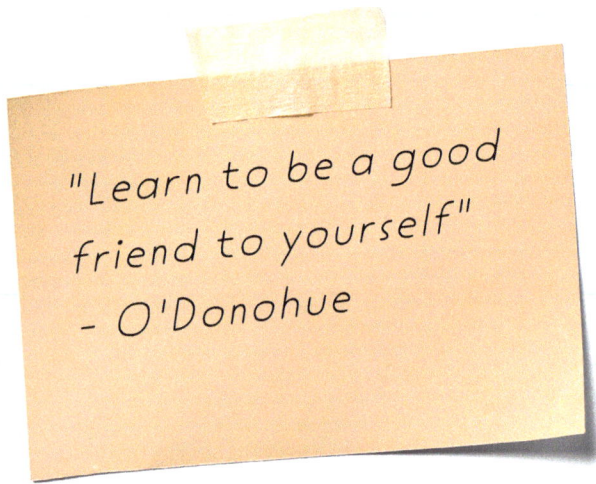

"Learn to be a good friend to yourself"
- O'Donohue

♥ Today someone told me I look agitated. I wasn't but I got why they would think that.

Wish or Weed?

♥ Today I got to the park late. I didn't hear a single frog. One of my favorite rituals each morning is to listen to the birds and frogs interacting by the willows. For whatever reason, the sound of the frogs' deep and monotone voices comforts me. I think it is helping me get used to a different sound.

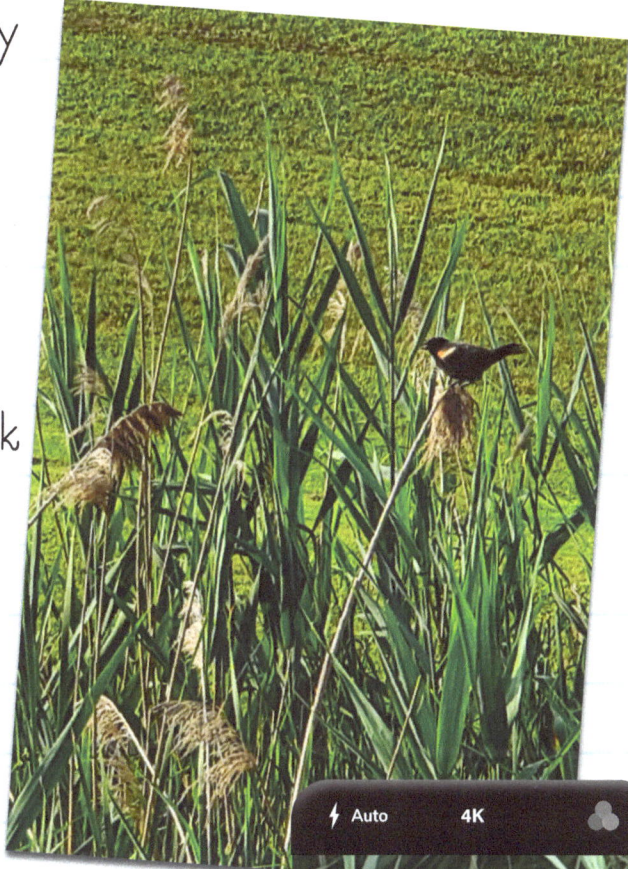

♥ Today I recorded the frogs and birds interacting so I can feel comforted when I need to.

♥ Today the park smelled different, but I don't know what it smelled like.

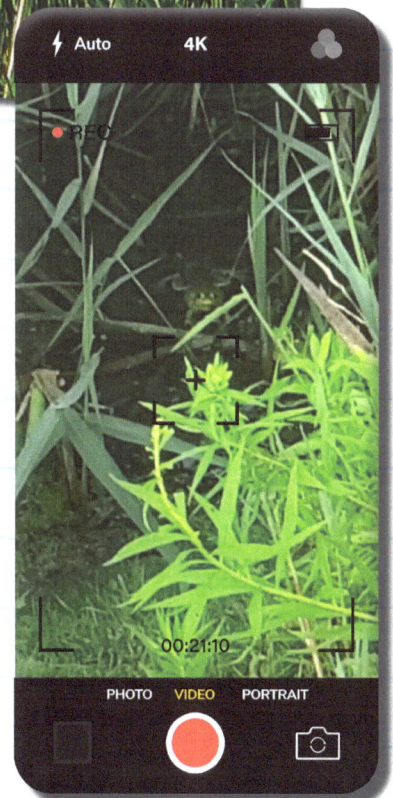

♥ Today as I was putting my shoes on while sitting on the front porch. I saw a baby flower in the corner. One I never saw before. It was so little, so I took a picture of it and enlarged it. I also sharpened the image so I could see its details more clearly. I wonder if it will grow.

♥ Today I came close to a bunny. It looked me in the eye, and I looked in its.

♥ Today I saw lots of little flowers and snapped photos of them too. I think this might become a new hobby.

♥ Today I felt like the flowers were talking to me.

in your
own
time

I know it feels like you're barely holding on

I GOT YOU

you got this

Be kind
to yourself

one step at a time

"You are such an interesting conversation" - Tuama

Today as I was peeking into the forest as I do daily, I saw a rake leaning against a tree. It is summer and the leaves are on the trees. The way it was standing there made it seem like someone placed it there.

"That which grows needs space" -O'Donohue

♥ Today I noticed that most of the trees in the park are leaning.

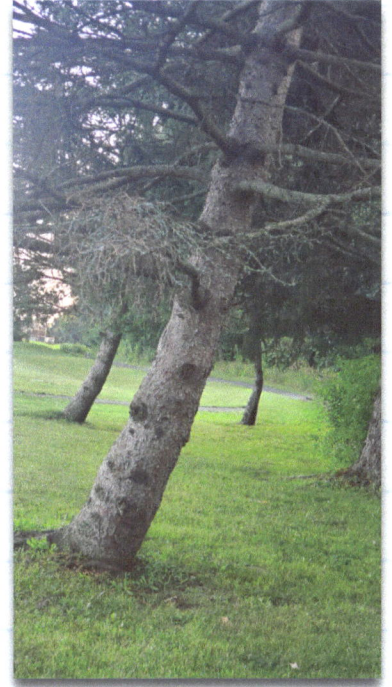

♥ Today I saw two deer, one on each side of the path. As I walked in the grass far around them, a younger runner stayed on the path and ran right between them. Why did I go around and why did they go between?

♥ My friend wrote a haiku. Today I decided to give one a try.

♥ Today I saw a heart tree and felt nurtured by nature.

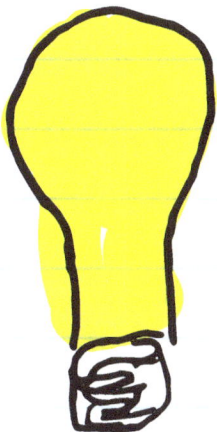

What if ?

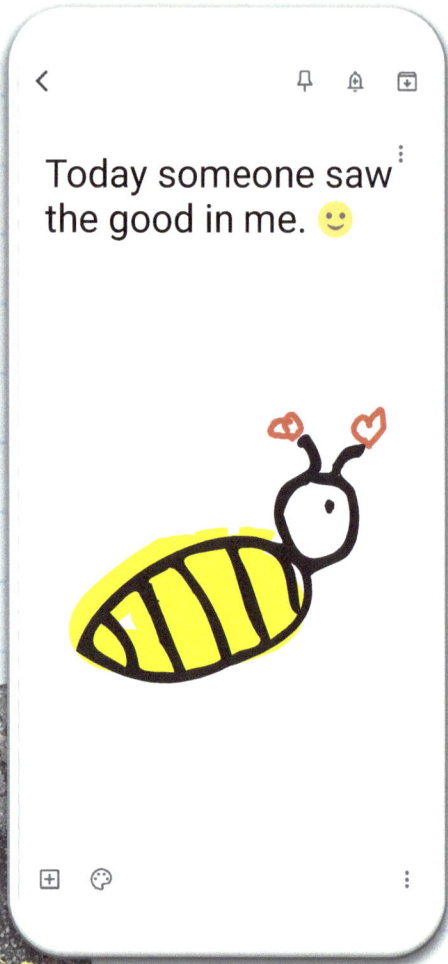

Today someone saw the good in me. 🙂

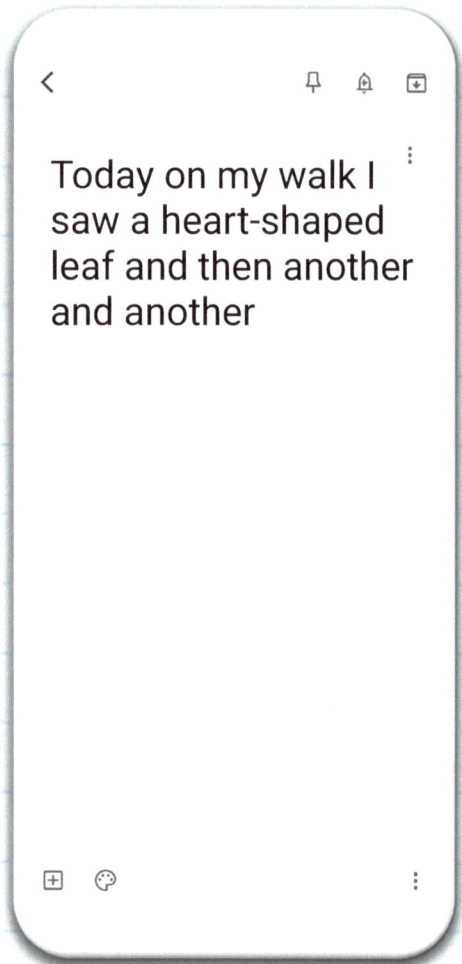

Today on my walk I saw a heart-shaped leaf and then another and another

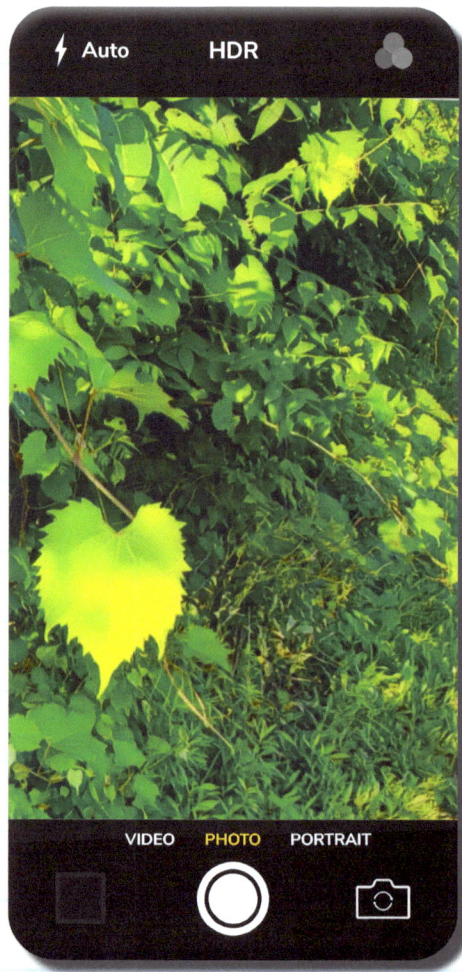

38

♥ Today I felt like the trees rolled out a red carpet for me. I really needed that.

♥ Today I heard a new song by Allison Russell. She uses the word **"WORTHY."** I think that is a word that shimmers!!

Empathy

♥ Today I thought about Pete the Cat.

♥ Today I bought myself school shoes. I chose heart shoes. I wrote a haiku too.

Read books and people
Like you, I wear my school shoes.
Learn grace. Uplift. Love.

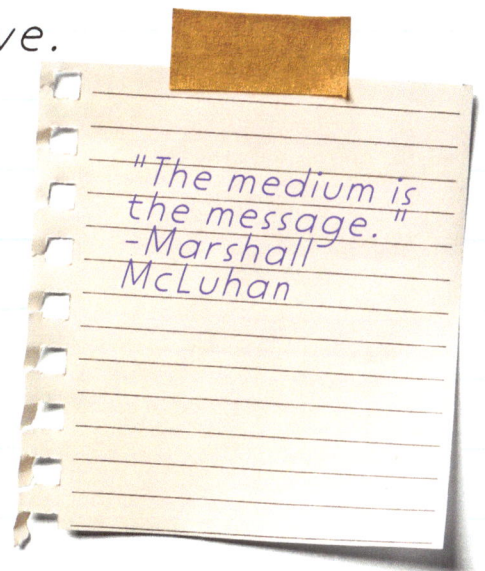

"The medium is the message."
-Marshall McLuhan

♥ Today I saw a rainbow and it wasn't raining. When I told others, most said something like "it had to be raining somewhere." I wondered if that was true.

"...learn to be friends with the earth and the sky, with the horizon and with the seasons, even with the disappearances of winter..." – Whyte

♥ Today I saw a heart on the ground at the park.

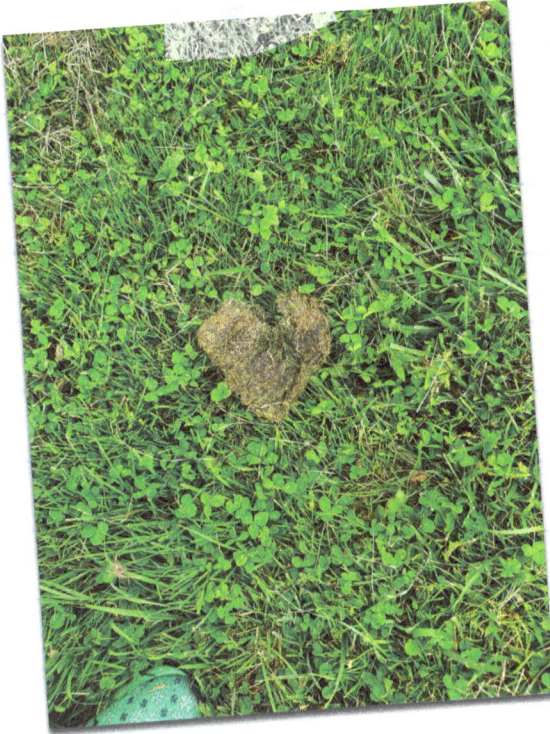

Today I noticed that you can transform a broken heart into wings. I wonder what else I can transform it into 🙂

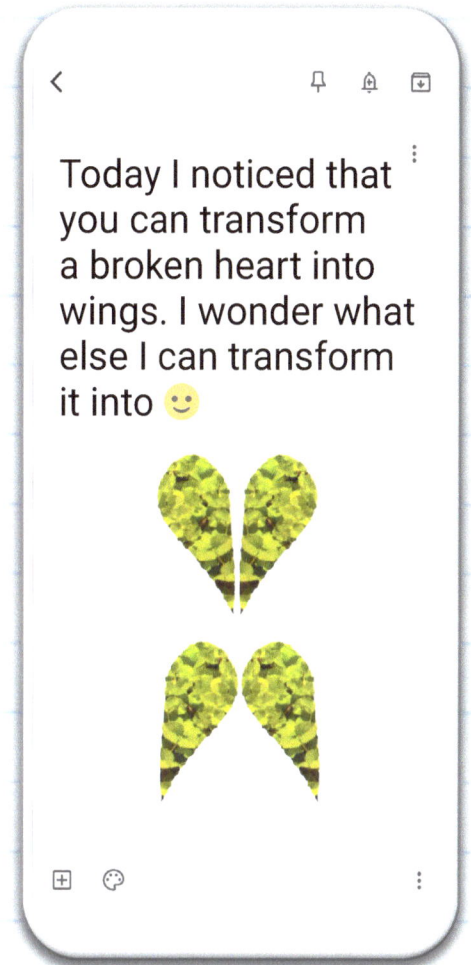

♥ Today I found the baby flower covered with light snow. Still thriving though.

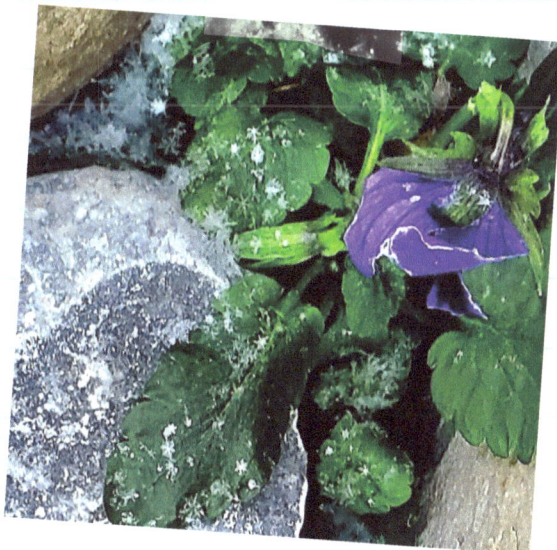

"When you see a rose open and beautiful, its very presence makes you feel wonderful." -Ruiz & Ruiz

♥ Today on my walk I listened to "The Bell and the Blackbird" poem. It tells the story about a monk who thought that both the sound of a bell and the sound of a blackbird are the most beautiful sounds.

♥ Today I thought to myself, I wish I had shoes with a heart on the bottom so I could leave hearts - or stars - or affirming words in the path. Maybe someone could create these. "Leave Your Mark" shoes.

♥ Today on the way to the park I saw a flower growing from a crack in the street. It looked like a bunch of baby grapes to me.

♥ Today I heard a new song called "Beautiful People." The singer said "I'd gather everyone together for a day and when we'd gather, I'd pass buttons out that say 'beautiful people.'"

♥ I started trying to create my own buttons.

"Give 'em what you got...You are a work of art"
- Tatiana Manaois

♥ Today I was listening to Taylor Swift's lyric "you can't spell awesome without me."

AWESOME!

♥ Today someone taught me the word "traverse" as a more inclusive term for walking.

♥ Today I wore my heart shoes because I knew I'd need a reminder to see the good, interact generously, pause before I speak, respect different opinions and ways of doing things, and remind myself that hurt is communicated differently by different people.

♥ Today my beautiful friend invited me to share joys and delights.

♥ Today at the park I came across something intriguing. Its heart shape and colorful mix grabbed my attention. From a distance it looked like a colorful heart in a puddle. My guess is that the combination of oil and water created the color. Some people say oil and water don't mix, but they sure do make something interesting, even **BEAUTIFUL**.

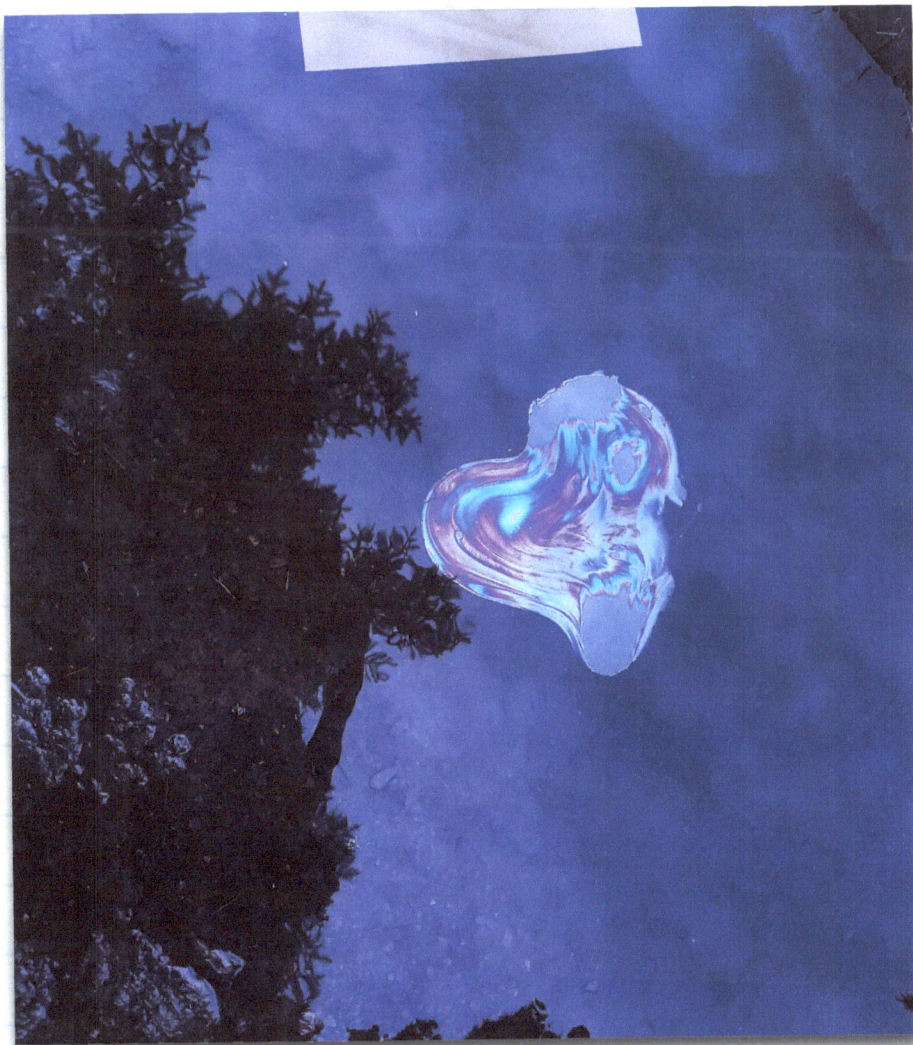

♥ Today I realized art is embedded in the word heart :-)

♥ Today I heard the sound of a squirrel. I didn't even know they made sounds. I guess I never really paid attention. Now I hear them often.

♥ Today I heard and saw geese fly over the willows.

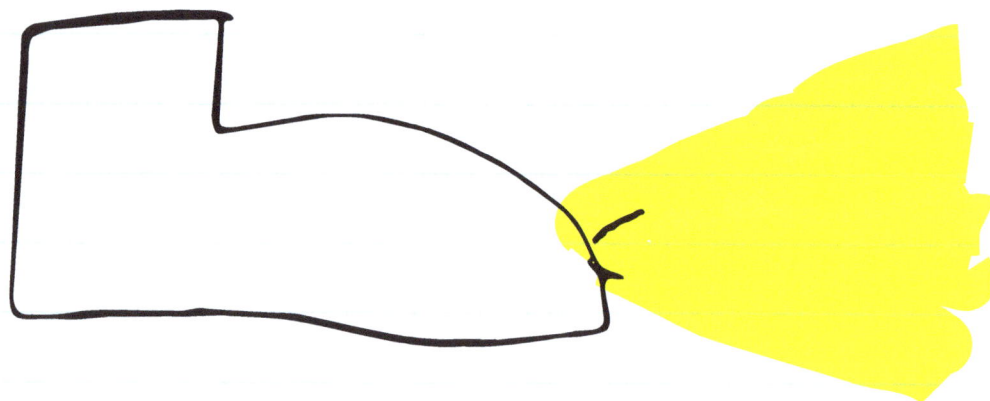

♥ Today I wished for light up shoes so I can see more clearly in the dark and so others could see me better too.

♥ Today on my walk I saw a person in front of me who reminded me of me - head down toward the phone, walking alone. They stepped aside for me. I stepped aside too and said thank you.

♥ Today I saw a flower cradling some kind of insect. It looked loving.

"...you matter, matter, MATTER." -Alicia Keys

♥ Today I listened to my work using earbuds and wondered if earbuds were named to reflect friendship or growth, or just their size.

♥ Today on my walk I wasn't sure who I wanted to listen to so I listened to myself.

♥ Today I passed someone on the path I had never seen before. They looked sad but that could have been the wrong interpretation. I looked them in the eye and said hello just in case. I think I'm expanding.

♥ Today I thought about all the beautiful gifts I saw when I was looking down.

♥ Today the sun and dew worked together to make the park glimmer.

♥ Today I wore red. I felt both empowered and loving.

♥ Today I learned that I like pastels. I didn't know that about myself.

Enlighten

♥ Today it looked like an artist painted the sky.

♥ Today, when I looked at the word traverse on paper, I noticed the word verse is embedded in it. Then I noticed it is also in "diverse."

Diverse

Traverse   Poetry

♥ Today I saw fog rising. It was beautiful.

♥ Today I saw my shadow and was reminded I'm not alone.

♥ Today I listened to a poem called "Yellow." It was written by Donna Ashworth. She said,

"Some people walk into your life with a light that can only be described as yellow infusing the very air around with the silent sound of this will be okay."

♥ Today I realized that the word "art" is in partner.

♥ Today I realized I was being unfair to someone. Always learning...

♥ Today I heard that "builders" are people whose mindset moves them to "create and to bring light to the world."

♥ Today I wondered if wonder woman was named "wonder woman" because she loved to wonder.

"When we let our light shine, we draw to us and are drawn to other BEARERS OF LIGHT"
-hooks

♥ Today on my walk I heard the song called "Better Days" and I thought about how much my story has shifted from when it first began. It has certainly been an unpredictable and interesting journey. I'm glad I gave myself time.

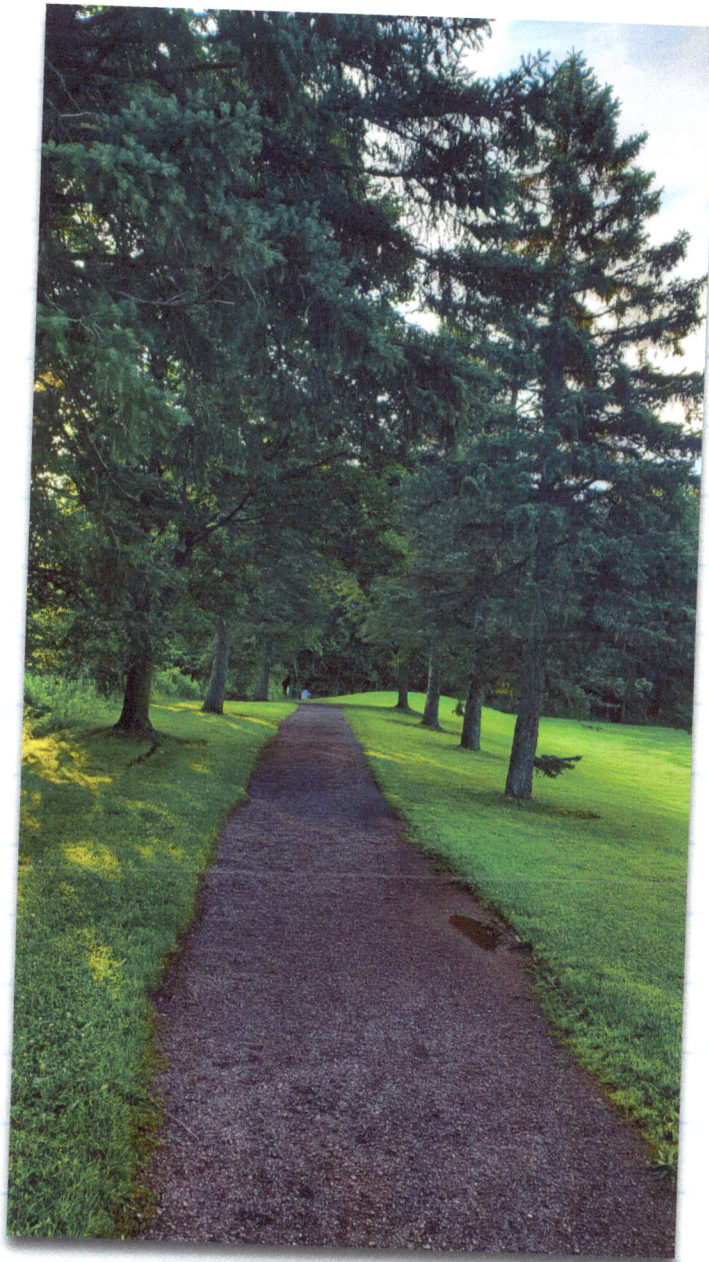

♥ Today as I stood at the top of the hill with one foot on the soft gravel and the other on the firm stone, as I do every day, I looked to the left and to the right noting color and light and beauty on both sides, even though the specific elements were different

♥ Today I felt like the flowers were talking to me again.

Make space

I see you

i got your back

be gentle

Be wild

♥ Today on my way to the park I was thankful for the small section of uneven ground that emerged from the center of a puddle and allowed me to cross the puddle without getting my sneakers wet. I don't think I ever noticed the unevenness before. When I took the picture, I realized that it looked like nothing. It made me wonder what other important things I haven't seen.

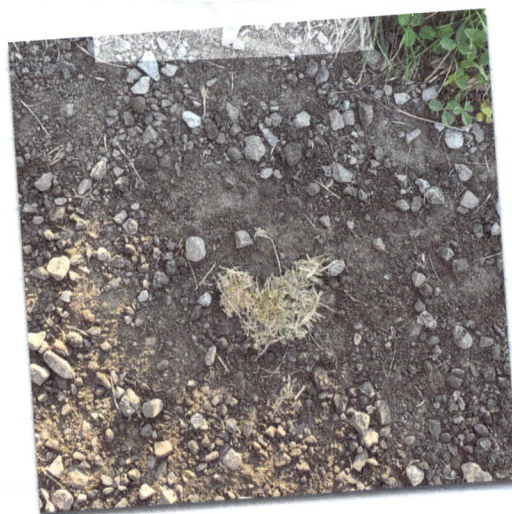

The Journey

♥ Today I heard a poet say

   "Pathmaker, there is no path.
   You make the path by walking.
   By walking, you make the path."

♥ Today I saw a pink cloud.

"Let them see your light, let it shine brightly, weirdly, wildly."
-Donna Ashworth

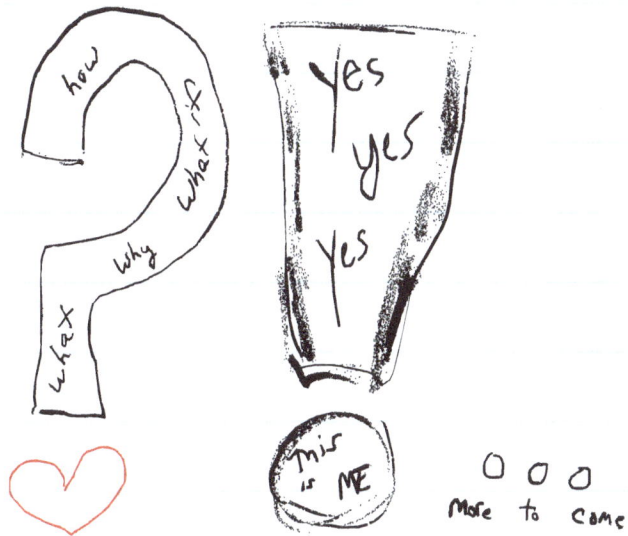

how what if
why
what

yes
yes
yes

this is ME

o o o
more to come

Merry

MORE ABOUT NOTEWORTHY

Dear Adult Reading Companions,

Thank you for engaging with *Noteworthy*. In this section, I share its backstory for those who are curious and interested. *Noteworthy* is one part of a larger project that attempts to capture the intricacy, complexity, and fluidity of a difficult experience. This experience stopped me in my tracks and then sent me on a journey I remain on today. It broke my heart into pieces and then helped me make a mosaic out of them. It brought me to the ground and taught me how to traverse differently. It challenged my communication and made me fall more in love with my profession as a communication professor. It transformed my role from a teacher to a student and then transformed my teaching. It opened my mind and my heart and expanded my policies and pedagogies. It made it hard to breathe and it inspired me.

On February 17, 2020, just three weeks before the pandemic spread chaos around the globe, a diagnosis of early-onset Parkinson's disease brought chaos to *my* world. In the moment of revelation, my doctor committed to doing everything they could to support my quality of life. They spoke about exercise and medication but, as a professor of communication, all I could think about was the wisdom I heard and echoed so many times in the classroom—*the quality of our lives is linked to the quality of our communication.*[1] Almost immediately I found myself experiencing the world very differently and not in a way that felt good to me. I looked in the mirror and didn't like what I was seeing. As poet and philosopher David Whyte shares, often the new you looking back appears as a stranger who we turn away from.

As a scholar with a longstanding interest in identity, difference, and connection, I understood why. I knew that communication is more than the transmission of information from one person to another; it is a symbolic process through which we create meanings and expectations for ourselves and others.

I also knew that meanings and expectations are not neutral. I knew that meanings can function to welcome, support, affirm, legitimize, and enable just as they can ostracize, constrain, invalidate, marginalize, and disable. What I then began learning was how it *feels* to experience the world as a person whose body differs from social and cultural expectations. Adding a layer of complexity was the fact that meanings and expectations *about communicating* were constraining me. Because the ability to use my hands was inconsistent throughout the day due to the symptoms of my disease, it became difficult for me to write, type, and even work a computer mouse. I also struggled with my nonverbal communication including body movements, vocal qualities, and facial expressions, which made being in front

1 John Stewart & Jody Koenig Kellas (2020) Co-constructing uniqueness: An interpersonal process promoting dialogue, *Atlantic Journal of Communication*, 28:1, 5–21, DOI: 10.1080/15456870.2020.1684289

of others uncomfortable for me. I struggled to move and to be still, to stand up straight, to speak clearly and with expression, and even to smile. These channels, which I had never critically examined before, now carried with them meanings, expectations, and judgments. I began to feel misunderstood, insecure, and lonely, as if everyone was staring but nobody was seeing me.

I knew the impact of illness extends far beyond the individual body. In other words, this illness would not just affect me. I had to figure out how to make friends with this new part of me for myself and for others—including my students and my family. I felt a strong need to do this before disclosing my illness publicly. To that end, I launched myself into a sensemaking journey. I started paying more mindful attention to my feelings and to the world around me, considering what I could do differently. Needing quiet to think, which was hard to find in a home that became a workplace and school due to the pandemic, I bought a pair of headphones to block out and to tune in. I started traversing physically, intellectually, and emotionally.

I spent many hours walking, often on a community park's circular path, immersed in conversations with scholars, musicians, philosophers, podcasters, poets, scientists, critics, spiritual teachers, and many others including myself. I documented everything that felt meaningful to me. In time, I started paying closer attention to the natural elements that surrounded me, which expanded the conversations and provided me with a new set of perspectives and benchmarks. In the park, with my headphones and notebook, I felt at ease and connected. It was as if I stumbled across a utopia or another world, or, perhaps better said, another world of meaning. I capture this positive experience in one of my earliest reflections.

> 5am. Awakened by the birds again. Calling to each other. Calling me. I get out of bed, tip toe downstairs, grab my shoes, and start walking toward the sun. I put my headphones on. Connected they tell me. The only thing that can help me. Some say escape. I say much more. I can't get them on fast enough, to block out the sound, the chaos surrounding me. Without them I can't think, I can't be. With them comes sound, but with this sound comes peace. The freedom to feel me, in all my complexity. They take me to a place others seem to have discovered before me. There, I can find what and only what I need. There, people seem to understand me. There, people care about the things that feel important to me. There, people support me. There I don't need to smile. There I don't need to worry. There I don't need to speak. There, I don't feel lonely.

I felt like I discovered a secret that I wanted to share with everyone. If it could do what it was doing for me, maybe it could do the same for others. With the help of colleagues, I attempted to capture the beauty of this experience in *Noteworthy*. What this version of *Noteworthy* doesn't showcase, however, is the significance my professional work had in my personal journey and how my personal journey catalyzed a desire to improve my teaching. I quickly noticed the interconnectedness between my professional work and my personal experience with each impacting the other positively.

During this time, I became engaged in professional initiatives related to diversity, equity, inclusion, belonging, and accessibility, which led me to many of the texts that engaged me so powerfully. This work also connected me with colleagues and students who, when in their presence, gave me the same feeling as being in the park with my headphones and notebook. These experiences and people all inspired me to try to create this feeling for myself and others, a feeling which I have come to refer to as spaciousness. Creating spaciousness required me to try new things, which I did slowly and cautiously. I started experimenting with new assignments, policies, pedagogical processes, classroom dynamics and more! *Noteworthy Expanded: Creating Spaciousness in Higher Education* captures this process in more detail and can be accessed using the QR code below. *Noteworthy Expanded* includes a more detailed notebook, substantial playlist, and examples of ways I tried to create spaciousness in courses and other aspects of my professional role.

To date, my journey, although difficult, was filled with beauty and inspiration and so many noteworthy moments. May your journeys be filled with inspiration and beauty.

In celebration,

Meredith

Access Ancillaries for Engaging with
Noteworthy in Elementary Learning
Environments online:
knightscholar.geneseo.edu/noteworthy/1/

Access *Noteworthy Expanded* online:
knightscholar.geneseo.edu/noteworthy/2/

Merry found comfort in music; here is her full playlist for you to explore!

Noteworthy Sources

"Don't ask the mountain / to move, just take a pebble / each time you visit."

> John Paul Lederach, "The Art of Peace," *On Being with Krista Tippett*, July 9, 2010, https://onbeing.org/programs/john-paul-lederach-the-art-of-peace/

"Don't worry, be happy"

> Bobby McFerrin, "Don't Worry, Be Happy" [song] in *Simple Pleasures* (Manhattan, 1988)

"When the silence isn't quiet and it feels like it's getting hard to breathe...I'll rise up, rise unafraid..."

> Cassandra Batie and Jennifer Decilveo, performed by Andra Day, "Rise Up" [song] on *Cheers to the Fall* (Buskin Records, 2015)

"It is loud in my mind today, jumbled up. I cannot think straight, no matter how many steps I take, everything feels so far away."

> Ashh Blackwood, "You're Gonna Be Okay" Extended Edition [song] in *You're Gonna Be Okay* (2022)

"Lend me your eyes and I'll change what you see."

> Mumford & Sons, "Awake My Soul" [song] on *Sigh No More* (Gentleman of the Road, 2009)

"When the fire inside that burns so bright begins to grow faded. It can be hard to see the ground on which you stand. Though you may not be afraid of walking in the darkness, you will feel like a stranger in this land."

> Brandi Carlile, Phil Hanseroth, and Tim Hanseroth, "This Time Tomorrow" [song] in *In These Silent Days* (Low Country Sound, 2021)

"Wish I could feel amazing, but this is all that I can feel today."

> Ed Sheeran, "Amazing" [song] in *Autumn Variations* (Gingerbread Man Records, 2023)

"Who will you be? What can you hear? Who are you now? What can you see?"

> Allison Russell, "Little Rebirth" [song] in *Outside Child* (Fantasy Records, 2021)

"Put down the weight of your aloneness and ease into the conversation"

> David Whyte, "Life at the Frontier: The Conversational Nature of Reality," TEDxPugetSound 2011, https://www.youtube.com/watch?v=5Ss1HuA1hIk=

"It's interestin' that nobody can walk in your shoes but still relate."

> NF, "Just Like You" [song] in *Clouds (The Mixtape)* (NF Real Music, 2021)

"When we recognize and accept our difficult feelings and emotions we begin to feel more at peace. When we see that mud is something that can help us grow we become less afraid of it."

Thích Nhất Hạnh, *The Art of Living* (HarperOne, 2017)

"The things that change us, if we notice, when we look up sometimes."

Alicia Keys, "Underdog" [song] in *Alicia* (RCA Records, 2020)

"I got a hammer, and I got a bell, and I got a song to sing all over this land, its the hammer of justice, it's a bell of freedom, it's a song about love…"

Pete Seeger and Lee Hays, performed by Peter, Paul, and Mary, "If I Had a Hammer" [song] in *Peter, Paul, and Mary* (Warner Brothers,1962)

"What can you do? What can be done?"

Allison Russell, "Little Rebirth" [song] in *Outside Child* (Fantasy Records, 2021)

"I'm gonna root, I'm gonna rise. I"m gonna dig, I'm gonna reach. Become a higher me."

Rob Riccardo, "Higher me" [song] in *Seeker* (2018)

"Help those who cross your path way, for they are there, and you came this way."

David V. White, *On Being Human* (Meaningful Life Books, 2013)

"What a world it would be if nature compared, if flowers didn't flower, because their neighbours were flowerier."

Donna Ashworth, poem "Youier…." In *Wild Hope (Black & White Publishing, 2021)*

"You belong among the wildflowers…You belong somewhere you feel free. "

Tom Petty, performed by The Wailin' Jennys, "Wildflowers" [song] in *Fifteen* (Festival, 2017)

"Look for the good"

Jason Mraz, Michael Goldwasser, Chaska Potter, Mai Sunshine Bloomfield, Mona Tavakoli, Rebecca Gebhardt, Abby Dorsey, and Jeff Berkley, performed by Jason Mraz, "Look for the Good" [song] in *Look for the Good* (Interrabang, 2020)

"Our job is to love the world"

Kate DiCamilo, "On Nurturing Capacious Hearts," *On Being with Krista Tippett*, March 17, 2022, https://onbeing.org/programs/kate-dicamillo-on-nurturing-capacious-hearts/

"We are billions of beautiful hearts"

P!nk, "What About Us" [song] in *Beautiful Trauma* (RCA, 2017)

"…may a flock of colours, indigo, red, green, and azure blue come to awaken in you a meadow of delight."

John O'Donohue, "Beannacht / Blessing" in *Anam Cara* (Harper Perennial, 1997)

"Stay gentle, the most powerful thing you can do."

Brandi Carlile, Phil Hanseroth, and Tim Hanseroth, performed by Brandi Carlile, "Stay Gentle" [song] in *In These Silent Days* (Low Country Sound, 2021)

"We're happy, free, confused, and lonely at the same time."

Taylor Swift, Max Martin, and Shellback, performed by Taylor Swift, "22 (Taylor's Version)" [song] in *Red (Taylor's Version)* (Republic, 2021)

"Sometimes all that you need is someone who can believe in you more than you do."

Andy Grammer, "Good in Me" [song] (S-Curve Records, 2022)

"...the seed...with the sun's love becomes the rose"

Amanda McBroom, performed by Bette Midler, The Rose [song] (Atlantic, 1980)

"When you touch a tree or sit at the foot of a tree, you can feel the energy of the tree pervading you. The tree has an energy. It simply stands there, being itself, and that is so refreshing, nourishing, and healing."

Thích Nhất Hạnh, *The Art of Living* (HarperOne, 2017)

"When we see other people who are in good communication with themselves and others, they inspire us."

Thích Nhất Hạnh, *The Art of Communicating* (HarperOne, 2013)

"Here's to the little ones who think they can touch the sun and ride on the moon to the stars...may they never put their wings away."

Kitty Oliver, "Don't Put Your Dreams Away" [song] in *The Calling of Our Time* (2013)

"Sunlight fell and reminded me that life can be so gracious sometimes and I felt like everything around me was connected somehow."

Hollow Coves, "Blessings" [song] in *Blessings* (2021)

"We can live in a world we design"

Benj Basek and Justin Paul, performed by P!nk, "A Million Dreams" [song] in *The Greatest Showman: Reimagined* (Atlantic, 2018)

"Whoever you are, no matter how lonely, the world offers itself to your imagination."

Mary Oliver, Poem "Wild Geese" in *Wild Geese* (Beacon Press, 1986), as heard on *On Being with Krista Tippett*, "On Listening to the World," April 3, 2020

"Use your imagination and a tremendous thing will happen."

Don Miguel Ruiz, *The Four Agreements: A Practical Guide to Personal Freedom* (Amber-Allen Publishing, 1997)

"I've been having revelations and I'm gon' let them shine."

Ben Darwish, Mandy Lee, Frans Mernick, and Cal Shapiro, performed by MisterWives, SUPERBLOOM [song] in *Superbloom* (Fueled by Ramen, 2020)

"Hey my little evening star, how bright you are."

Allison Russell, performed by Allison Russell and Brandi Carlile, "You're Not Alone" [song] (Fantasy Records, 2022)

"The world needs you now. You matter, matter, matter."

Alicia Keys, "Good Job" [song] in *Alicia* (RCA Records, 2020)

"You are a work of art."

Tatiana Manaois, "Like You" [song] in *Like You* (2015)

"Self-love is crucial for loving others."

Thích Nhất Hạnh, *The Art of Communicating* (HarperOne, 2013)

"To love ourselves and others will depend on the presence of a loving environment."

bell hooks, *All About Love: New Visions* (William Morrow Paperbacks, 2000)

"Let your community be you and be your community."

Thích Nhất Hạnh, *The Art of Communicating* (HarperOne, 2013)

"Anything you do for yourself, you are also doing for the world."

Thích Nhất Hạnh, *The Art of Living* (HarperOne, 2017)

"Now's your chance to dance."

Etienne Bowler, Mandy Lee, Frans Mernick, and Adam Palin, performed by MisterWives, "Decide to Be Happy" [song] in *Superbloom* (Fueled by Ramen, 2020)

"People are just as wonderful as sunsets if I can let them be..."

Carl Rogers, "Experiences in Communication" In *Bridges not Walls: A Book about Interpersonal Communication* 9th edition (McGraw-Hill, 2005). Edited by John Stewart.

"Learn to be a good friend to yourself"

John O'Donohue, "A Friendship Blessing" in *Anam Cara* (Harper Perennial, 1997)

"If no one ever hears it, how we gonna learn your song? They can read all about it"

Emeli Sandé, Professor Green, Iain James, Tom Barnes, Ben Kohn, and Pete Kelleher, performed by Emeli Sandé "Read All About It, Pt. III" [song] in *Our Version of Events* (Virgin, 2012)

"You are such an interesting conversation"

Pádraig Ó Tuama, "How to ~~Belong~~ Be Alone," in *Dumbo Feather*, January 3, 2020, featured on *The On Being Project*, November 2, 2020, https://onbeing.org/poetry/how-to-be-alone/

"That which grows needs space"

John O'Donohue, *Anam Cara* (Harper Perennial, 1997)

"The medium is the message."

Marshall McLuhan

"Worthy"

Allison Russell, Drew Lindsay and JT Nero, performed by Allison Russell, "The Returner" [song] in *The Returner* (Fantasy Records, 2023)

"...learn to be friends with the earth and the sky, with the horizon and with the seasons, even with the disappearances of winter..."

David Whyte, *Consolations* Revised Edition (Many Rivers Press, 2021)

"When you see a rose open and beautiful, its very presence makes you feel wonderful"

Don Miguel Ruiz and Don Jose Ruiz, *The Fifth Agreement* (Amber-Allen Publishing, 2010)

"The Bell and the Blackbird"

David Whyte, "The Bell and the Blackbird," *The Bell and the Blackbird* (Many Rivers Press, 2018), as heard in "David Whyte: Poetry From the On Being Gathering (Opening Night)," *On Being with Krista Tippett*, September 10, 2018, https://onbeing.org/programs/poetry-from-the-on-being-gathering-david-whyte-opening-night-sep2018/

"I'd gather everyone together for a day and when we'd gather, I'd pass buttons out that say 'beautiful people.'"

Melanie Safka, "Beautiful People," Melanie (Buddah, 1969)

"Give 'em what you got...You are a work of art"

Tatiana Manaois, "Like You" [song] in *Like You* (2015)

"You can't spell 'awesome' without ME"

Taylor Swift, Joel Little, and Brendan Urie, performed by Taylor Swift and Brendan Urie, "Me!" [song] in *Lover* (Republic, 2019)

"...you matter, matter, matter."

Alicia Keys, "Good Job" [song] in *Alicia* (RCA Records, 2020)

"Some people walk into your life with a light that can only be described as yellow infusing the very air around with the silent sound of this will be okay."

Donna Ashworth, "Yellow," *Growing Brave* (Mango, 2024)

"...builders [are people whose mindset moves them to] create and to bring light to the world."

Daniel Lubetsky, "Why the world needs more builders—and less 'us vs. them'" TED2024, https://www.ted.com/talks/daniel_lubetzky_why_the_world_needs_more_builders_and_less_us_vs_them

"When we let our light shine, we draw to us and are drawn to other bearers of light"

bell hooks, *All About Love* (William Morrow Paperbacks, 2000)

"Better Days"

Dermot Kennedy, Samuel Romans, Scott Harris, Daniel Nigro, and Carey Willetts, as performed by Dermot Kennedy, "Better Days" [song] in *Sonder* (Riggins Recording, 2022)

"Let them see your light, let it shine brightly, weirdly, wildly."

Donna Ashworth, "Moths" in *Life, Love and Loss* (Black & White Publishing, 2021)

"Pathmaker, there is no path. / You make the path by walking. / By walking, you make the path."

Antonio Machado, "Caminante, no hay camino..." from "Proverbios y cantares" in *Campos de Castilla* (1917), as heard in "David Whyte: Poetry From the On Being Gathering (Opening Night)," *On Being with Krista Tippett*, September 10, 2018, https://onbeing.org/programs/poetry-from-the-on-being-gathering-david-whyte-opening-night-sep2018/

ACKNOWLEDGMENTS

Among the many lessons I learned during this first part of my journey is that help is both necessary and beautiful.

Allison—your organizational and creative brilliance amazes me. You are so good at what you do. I am incredibly grateful for the time, care, and energy you invested into this project and for your continuous patience throughout the process.

Patrick—your artistic talent and vision brought me so much joy. Each illustration was a priceless gift as were the conversations they generated.

Thank you both for listening lovingly, giving generously, and providing me the opportunity to experience the magic of dialogic synergy.

To those who supported this work as reviewers. Your thoughtful, encouraging, and honest feedback invited me to go deeper and reach higher. Thank you for making the work better and my journey more growth enhancing.

To the Geneseo Foundation, Inc. for the generous financial support in the form of Incentive Grants and Publication Award.

To the Rochester Regional Library Council for the generous financial support in the form of a RRLC Special Projects Grant.

To those who contributed a pebble to my path: you shone your light to help me find mine, showed me the beauty of uniqueness, modeled kind, positive, and compassionate communication, and brought delight to my day. And, to those who journeyed with me in friendship: thank you for helping me traverse more lovingly in my own shoes.

To those who shared tools to help me sow new seeds, many of which came from the following SUNY Geneseo initiatives and programs:

- Cultivating Community
- Advancing Cultural Competency Certification
- President's Commission for Diversity and Community
- Intergroup Dialogue Program
- ECHC Think Tank
- Belonging Dialogues

To those who did it all. There aren't enough beautiful words. Please know that I will be forever grateful.

To those who care for the park. Thank you for providing me a beautiful place to traverse.

To my family, thank you for being there each time I returned.

ABOUT THE AUTHOR

Meredith Harrigan (she/her, Ph.D., University of Nebraska-Lincoln) is a Professor in the Department of Communication at the State University of New York College at Geneseo where she teaches courses in interpersonal, family, organizational, cultural, and dialogic communication.

Dr. Harrigan is committed to understanding the myriad ways communication matters in people's lives. Of particular interest to her is how individuals communicatively negotiate personal, professional, and relational identities within and across a variety of contexts. Her individual and collaborative research, which is guided by interpretive and critical theories, can be found in various outlets including *Journal of Family Communication*, *Journal of Applied Communication Research*, *Journal of Social and Personal Relationships*, and *Journal of Diversity in Higher Education*.

Dr. Harrigan brings her knowledge of relationship-building and passion for dialogic communication to her service by co-coordinating the College's Cultivating Community Program.

She is a 2016 recipient of the Chancellor's Award for Excellence in Teaching and a 2023 recipient of Geneseo's Diversity and Inclusion Leadership Award.

In addition to walking, Dr. Harrigan enjoys attending her children's athletic events and musical concerts, chasing rainbows, and photographing delightful moments and discoveries.

ABOUT THE ILLUSTRATOR

Patrick Montanaro is a Rochester-based illustrator with a preference for concept art, fantasy illustrations, children's books, and comics. His roots in pen-and-ink maintain its traditional grit as he explores dynamic and digital storytelling with a hand-drawn feel. Past collaborators include the musical group Transviolet, Aaron Celentano, as well as various comic and film productions in need of imaginative worldbuilding and character-driven visuals. Patrick's interest in gesture and form was sparked by years spent observing martial artists and bodybuilders—an influence that gives his characters their signature energy and presence.

*A*long with a great deal of collaboration and inspiration from Meredith Harrigan and Patrick Montanaro, this book was designed and typeset by Allison P. Brown using Adobe InDesign. Main story text is set in Spectral designed by Production Type and is open source, Merry's handwriting in Tomarik (Extrovert) and the cover and title text in Tomarik (Poster) both designed by Mariya Lish, the lyrics Merry hears in the park in Carrotflower designed by Crystal Kluge, and text Merry reads in Typeka designed by E-Lan Ronen.

The author, illustrator, and publisher give this book freely in the spirit of education, gratitude, and generosity.

"When you learn, teach. When you get, give."
Maya Angelou.

We hope you will take what you need from this story, listen to flowers, and know you matter.

www.ingramcontent.com/pod-product-compliance
Lightning Source LLC
Chambersburg PA
CBHW042013080426
42734CB00003B/64